Book brief

1. This is the true story of the writer as a boy when he was bullied at school.

2. Michael likes school and is a clever boy, but he doesn't like going to school because of the bullies.

3. He has a 'special friend', Andrew, who helps him in his most difficult moments.

4. Then Michael makes friends with David, and an old man, Tom, and things start to change for the better.

5. These new friends help Michael to believe in himself and, most of all, to like himself.

www.eligradedreaders.com

In this reader:

 **21st Century Skills**	To encourage students to connect the story to the world they live in.	
Key	A2 level activities.	
Story Notes	A brief summary of the text.	
Glossary	Explanation of difficult words.	
Picture Caption	A brief explanation of the picture.	
Audio	These icons indicate the parts of the story that are recorded.	start ■ stop
Think	To encourage students to develop their critical thinking skills.	

Michael Lacey Freeman

Egghead

Activities by
Sarah Gudgeon

Illustrated by
Zosja Dzierzawska

Teen Eli Readers

The **ELI Readers** collection is a complete range of books and plays for readers of all ages, ranging from captivating contemporary stories to timeless classics. There are four series, each catering for a different age group: **First ELI Readers, Young ELI Readers, Teen ELI Readers** and **Young Adult ELI Readers**. The books are carefully edited and beautifully illustrated to capture the essence of the stories and plots. The readers are supplemented with 'Focus on' texts packed with background cultural information about the writers and their lives and times.

Egghead
by Michael Lacey Freeman
Language Level Consultant
Silvana Sardi
Illustrated by **Zosia Dzierzawska**

ELI Readers
Founder and Series Editors
Paola Accattoli, Grazia Ancillani, Daniele Garbuglia (Art Director)

Graphic Design
**Andersen
the Premedia Company**

Production Manager
Francesco Capitano

Photo credits
Shutterstock

New edition: **2021**
First edition: **2016**

© **ELI s.r.l.**
**P.O. Box 6
62019 Recanati (MC)
Italy**
T **+39 071750701**
F **+39 071977851**
**support@elipublishing.com
www.elipublishing.com**

Typeset in 12 / 17 pt
Fulmar designed by Leo Philp

Printed in Italy by
**Tecnostampa - Pigini Group
Printing Division
Loreto - Trevi (Italia) -
ERT 246.10
ISBN 978-88-536-3203-6**

Contents

6	**Main Characters**	
8	**Before you read**	
10	**Chapter 1**	*The Monster Horse*
18	**Activities**	
20	**Chapter 2**	*A Day at School*
28	**Activities**	
30	**Chapter 3**	*Egg and Bacon and the Invisible Ball*
38	**Activities**	
40	**Chapter 4**	*The Old Man*
48	**Activities**	
50	**Chapter 5**	*Tom's Story*
58	**Activities**	
60	**Chapter 6**	*The Prize*
68	**Activities**	
70	**Focus on...**	*Michael Lacey Freeman*
72	**Focus on...**	*Bullying*
74	**Focus on...**	*School in Britain*
76	**Focus on...**	*London - Places*
78	**Test Yourself**	
79	**Syllabus**	

Main Characters

Michael   **Andrew**

This is Michael with his 'special friend', Andrew, who he talks to in his head. Michael, the author if this book, is bullied at school, but Andrew helps him in his most difficult moments.

Mum   **Tom**

Michael's mum is happy when she sees Michael happy.   *An old man who Michael becomes friends with. He helps Michael to realise that what the bullies say isn't important because they don't really know him.*

David

David is bullied like Michael at school. The two become friends.

Mrs Hewitt

Michael's new English teacher. She understands Michael better than his other teachers.

Kevin **Clive**

Two bullies who call Michael horrible names and won't let him play with them and the other boys.

Before you read

Grammar

1 Read about the story and choose the correct word (s).

Egghead is a story about a boy called Michael who *leaves / lives* near London. He's good (**1**) *at / of* school, but he doesn't like (**2**) *go / going* there. The other children bully him. They call him, 'Egghead'. But Michael (**3**) *has / have* a special friend (**4**) *who / which* helps him when he goes (**5**) *at / to* school. This boy's name's Andrew. Andrew isn't like other boys. (**6**) Nobody *can to see / can see* Andrew. In fact, Andrew isn't a real boy. He's inside Michael's head.

Vocabulary

2 Match these words used in the story with their definitions.

1 ☐ school assembly
2 ☐ break time
3 [a] classroom
4 ☐ headteacher
5 ☐ playground
6 ☐ canteen

a where the students do their lessons.
b where the students play.
c where all the students at the school meet.
d where students have lunch.
e when students have a rest in between lessons.
f the most important person in the school.

3 Rearrange the letters to see what Michael studies at school.

CHERFN _FRENCH_
1 SHLGNEI _____
2 TRA _____
3 TOSIHYR _____
4 OGGRAPHYE _____
5 CENCEIS _____

Pair Work

4 Put the words in the correct order to make sentences about bullying. Then talk to your partner about what you can do if you see someone bullied in these ways.

me names call they. – *they call me names.*
1 with me never they to play want.
2 hit they me and hurts it.
3 don't to me speak they.
4 post they comments horrible online.
5 send emails that my hurt they feelings.

Reading A2 Key

5 Complete the first part of the story with the missing words.

Hello. My name _is_ Michael, but everyone calls me 'Egghead' (**1**) _____ school. It's true, my head (**2**) _____ bigger than anyone else's and my body is quite small. Everyone agrees that it's (**3**) _____ right name for me. That's why I don't like going (**4**) _____ school. The other children call me this name (**5**) _____ the time. They're horrible to me, and make (**6**) _____ feel bad.

Chapter 1

The Monster Horse

▶2 *January 1973*

Hello. My name's Michael, but everyone calls me 'Egghead' at school. It's true, my head is bigger than anyone else's and my body is quite small. Everyone agrees that it's the right name for me. The other children call me this name all the time.

That's why I don't like going to school. The children in my class are horrible to me, and make me feel bad. They never call me Michael. They always call me, 'Egghead.'

But I'm lucky. I've got a friend who I talk to all the time. He's not real. I can't touch[1] him or see him. Nobody can see him. He's invisible[2]. He's inside my head, you see. His name's Andrew, and he helps me. Nobody else knows about Andrew. He's my secret[3] friend. He's the only one who doesn't call me Egghead. He hasn't even got a head because he lives inside mine.

Andrew is my best friend. He always tries to help me. When I have a problem, I ask Andrew what I can do. He tried to help me at school the other day.

'Our class is going to read a poem for the school

> At school they call Michael 'Egghead' because he has a big head. They're horrible to him, but Michael has an invisible friend, Andrew, who helps him.

---
[1] **touch** feel with your hands
[2] **invisible** something that nobody can see
[3] **secret** something you don't tell other people

Egghead

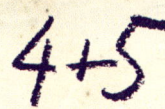

assembly next week,' said our English teacher, Miss White. 'The headteacher will be there. One of you can read it to everybody in the school. It's called, 'The Monster Horse,' and it's by Ian Serrailer. Who would like to read it?'

'Do it! Do it!' said Andrew. 'You can do it. I know you can.'

My hand went up. 'Miss, Miss, I'll do it,' I said. I liked reading.

Then I could hear people in the class laughing.

'No, Egghead can't do it. I'll do it,' said Stephen Foster.

'Well,' said Miss White. 'You can't both read it. I know, why don't you both read it now? Then the class will decide which one is the best.' Bad idea, Miss White.

I had to speak first. 'Read it as if you're a horse,' said Andrew. So, that's what I did. I read all the poem like a horse.

'Theeeee Mooonsteeer Hooooorse byyyy Ian Serraileeerrr.'

Now I could hear more people in the class laughing. Miss White told them to be quiet. But when people start

Andrew tells Michael to read the poem as if he were a horse. Everybody in the class laughs at him.

Michael Lacey Freeman

laughing, it's difficult to stop them. In fact[1], if you tell them to stop, they laugh even more.

When I finished, Stephen Foster read the poem. It was boring. He read it in a normal voice. He didn't try to sound like a horse at all.

'Thank you, Michael, thank you Stephen,' said Miss White. 'Now let's decide. Who do you want to read the poem? Hands up who wants Michael to read it.' My hand went up. I looked around the class. Nobody else put up their hand.

The teacher looked a little bit confused[2]. At first, she didn't know what to say. 'OK er...' she said, 'What about Stephen?'

Everybody except me put their hand up.

'Hooray' shouted the class.

'Down with Egghead!' shouted a boy.

'Quiet,' said Miss White again. 'That's decided then. Stephen will read the poem at the school assembly.' Miss White could see my face. I was trying not to, but I was about to cry. I remembered what my dad said, and what Peter said in my favourite book, *The Railway Children*, "Big boys don't cry."

'I think that Michael, you did so well, why don't you

Everyone in the class chooses the other boy to read the poem at assembly, even though Michael read it better. Michael tries not to cry.

Everyone except Michael puts their hand up because they want the other boy, not Michael, to read the poem to all the school.

[1] **in fact** actually
[2] **confused** you feel this when you don't know what to say or do

Michael Lacey Freeman

In the end, the teacher says Michael can read the title of the poem. He's happy about this and Andrew tells him he's very good when he reads it at assembly.

read the title[1] of the poem at the assembly,' said Miss White.

The class started laughing again, but I didn't feel unhappy this time. Andrew was right. Now I was able to read, at least the first bit of the poem. The title. That really is the most important bit. Without the title you have no idea what the poem is going to be about.

So, thanks to Andrew I read the title at the school assembly, in front of the whole school. Even the headteacher was there, smiling.

'Theeeee Mooonsteeer Hooooorse,' byyyy Ian Serraileeerrrrr. That little bit. And then Stephen read the rest. Andrew thought I was very, very good.

Michael likes his art teacher. He didn't know how to draw before Mr Wilson taught him a simple way to draw a picture.

Mr Wilson teaches us art. He's very old. He's got white hair, and he wears a big winter jumper, even when it's really hot. I like him very much. He teaches us to draw. Drawing seemed so difficult before I met Mr Wilson. He taught me to draw this picture. All you have to do is draw the number 3, and then add a line to the top part of the number. Then you add some more lines, some going up and some going down. After this you just have to add a few more things, like a boat, and the sun, and that's it. Can you see what it's?

Can you see a boy on the cliff[2]? That's me. I'm

This is Michael's picture. He likes his art teacher because he teaches them how to draw in a simple way.

---

[1] **title** the name of a poem or a story
[2] **cliff** look where I'm standing on page 15

Michael Lacey Freeman

Michael loves reading even more than drawing because when he reads he forgets about being an egghead. He also plays football by himself at home with a balloon for the ball.

reading my favourite book, *The Railway Children*. One thing I like even more than drawing is reading. I spend a lot of time in my bedroom, reading books like *Treasure Island*, *Anne of Green Gables*, *Robinson Crusoe* and *Gulliver's Travels*. When I read these books, I forget that I'm an egghead. I live inside the story.

I love my books. They always tell you the same story. But you can add things to it. You can imagine[1] that you're there as well, looking for secrets, or discovering[2] an island. Andrew is always there with me as well.

I also play football by myself. I'm both teams. My bedroom door is one goal, and the kitchen door is the other goal. All the different teams play, except England, of course. How can I be both teams if England play? England will always win.

Freeman has the ball, he passes to Andrew, Andrew shoots, Gooaaaalllllll!!!!

I use a balloon when I play, so I don't break anything and I only play when my Mum and Dad are out.

I never tell Mum and Dad about school. I want to tell them, but I don't want them to know that all the other children call me Egghead. Then maybe they'll call me Egghead as well. So, it's a secret, just between me and Andrew.

[1] **imagine** if you imagine something, you see it in your head
[2] **discover** find

Egghead

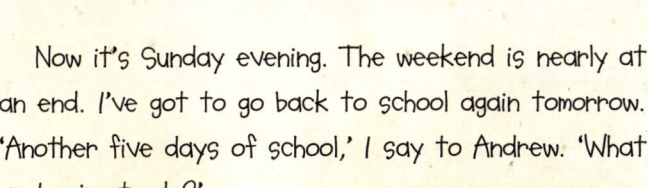

Now it's Sunday evening. The weekend is nearly at an end. I've got to go back to school again tomorrow. 'Another five days of school,' I say to Andrew. 'What am I going to do?'

'Don't worry,' says Andrew. 'I'll be there with you. Everything will be OK.'

'Thank you Andrew,' I say. I try not to worry, but it isn't easy.

Every Sunday evening, Mum makes me a hot chocolate drink and she lets me watch, *Planet of the Apes* on TV. It's always a special moment. But, even though[1] I really enjoy it, I can't stop thinking about school. Tomorrow I'll have to go back to that place. I can't wait to be old like Mum and Dad. Then I can stay at home, read my books, play football, and watch the TV as much as I want.

> Michael's mum and dad don't know that they call him Egghead at school. On Sunday, Michael is worried about going back to school. In his head, Andrew tells him not to worry, but it isn't easy.

Think
Do you think Michael should tell his parents about how unhappy he is at school? Why / Why not?

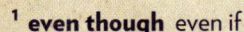
[1] **even though** even if

After-reading Activities • Chapter 1

Reading Comprehension

1 Look at these sentences about Michael. Tick (✓) the ones that you think are true.

- ✓ Michael is called 'Egghead' at school.
- 1 ☐ He doesn't like going to school.
- 2 ☐ He didn't want to read the poem.
- 3 ☐ He read the poem at the school assembly.
- 4 ☐ He likes drawing.
- 5 ☐ His favourite book is *Treasure Island*.
- 6 ☐ He plays football with Andrew.
- 7 ☐ His mum and dad don't know about Andrew.

2 Match the questions with the answers.

- 1 [c] Why does Michael feel lucky?
- 2 ☐ Why doesn't Michael like school?
- 3 ☐ Why doesn't Michael like the way Stephen reads the poem?
- 4 ☐ How does Michael read the poem?
- 5 ☐ What does Michael think is the most important part of the poem?
- 6 ☐ What does Michael do on Sunday evenings?

- a He thinks it's boring.
- b He drinks a hot chocolate.
- c Because he has a special friend.
- d Because the other children bully him.
- e He reads it like a horse.
- f The title.

Speaking and Writing

3 **In Chapter 1, Michael says he loves reading. Answer these questions about you and then write your answers.**

1. Where do you usually read?
2. What kind of books do you like reading? Why?
3. How important do you think it is to read books?
4. Do you prefer reading paper books or ebooks?
5. What's the best book you've ever read?
6. How often do you go to the library?
7. Where do you usually look for information online?

Before-reading Activity

Listening A2 Key

▶ 3 **4** **Listen to the start of Chapter 2 and choose the correct answer (A, B or C) for each question.**

On Monday morning it was
A sunny.   **B** foggy.   **C** windy.

1. Who does Michael say hello to?
   A His teacher   **B** His dad   **C** An old man
2. Where does Michael sometimes go with his dad?
   A To the woods   **B** To the mountains   **C** To the beach
3. What kind of shop does Mrs Jarvis have?
   A A shoe shop   **B** A sweet shop   **C** A supermarket
4. How did Michael feel when he saw that the school was still there?
   A Really excited   **B** Very surprised   **C** He wanted to cry
5. One of the boys asks Michael if he was in the ____ at the weekend.
   A zoo   **B** cinema   **C** park

Chapter 2

A Day at School

▶ 3 *February 1973*

It's Monday morning! I hate going to school. I have to walk up this big hill and I feel quite lonely¹. This morning it was very foggy, and I couldn't see much in front of me.

I felt better when I saw that the old man was there. Halfway up the hill there's an old man who always sits on the same bench². He wears a hat and he has a very big grey moustache. He has a kind face, and he always says hello to me.

'Hello, Cherub³,' he said.

'Hello,' I said. 'It's very foggy today.'

'Yes, it is,' he said. 'Be careful you don't fall down. I have to be careful. That's why I've got this walking stick⁴.'

When I'm older I want to have a walking stick. Then I can use it when I go for a walk in the woods. I love the woods. Sometimes my dad takes me. He always pretends⁵ that we're lost. I know we're not lost really. Dad knows the woods really well, but I pretend we're lost as well. It's very exciting.

Michael hates going to school and today it's foggy. He always speaks to an old man with a walking stick. Sometimes he goes for a walk in the woods with his dad and they play at being lost.

¹ **lonely** without friends
² **bench** where the old man is sitting on page 47
³ **cherub** little
⁴ **walking stick** this helps people to walk
⁵ **pretend** act as if something is real but you know it isn't

Egghead

After speaking to the old man, I went to the sweet shop. The lady there is always nice to me. I didn't want any sweets. I just wanted to say hello.

'Hello, Mrs Jarvis,' I said.

'Hello, dear,' she said. 'Put your hat and scarf on. It's very cold out there.'

'OK, Mrs Jarvis,' I said. I put my hat and scarf on and went out again. I felt quite good now. I belonged. This was my street and nobody called me names here, or made me feel small and stupid.

When I got to the top of the hill, the school was near. Then I stopped feeling happy. I looked around, but I couldn't see the school. I couldn't see it because of the fog. 'Maybe it's not there anymore,' I thought. I started to pray. 'Please God. Take the school away. Make it go away,' I said. I walked down the road to school. I still couldn't see it. I got nearer and nearer, and nearer and nearer, and then ... I saw it. The school was still there. I wanted to cry but I didn't. I had to be strong. 'Maybe today will be better.' I thought.

But it wasn't. It started as soon as I went into the classroom.

'Oh no, it's Egghead,' said Kevin.

After speaking to the old man and the woman in the sweet shop, Michael feels better. It's so foggy, he can't see the school and he hopes it's gone forever.

School is still there, of course, and so are the bullies who call him Egghead.

Michael Lacey Freeman

'I didn't see your ugly face this weekend,' said Clive. 'Where were you? At the zoo?' The other boys and girls in the class laughed. I don't know why. It wasn't funny at all.

'Quiet,' said Miss White. 'Today we're going to do some exercises about...'

▶ 4 'Don't listen to them,' said Andrew. 'Just do what Miss White says. Don't listen to Kevin or Clive. They don't know what they're talking about.'

▶ 5 Lessons were quite easy. I didn't have to work too hard. I always knew the answers to Miss White's questions. I didn't always answer her though[1]. I didn't want the other boys and girls to notice[2] me. I finished the exercises very quickly. Then I waited for everybody else to finish. While I waited, I looked out of the window. 'How I'd like to be in the woods now,' I thought. 'Or at home reading my book. Or talking to the old man.' But here I was in this classroom, waiting for the lesson to end.

After half an hour Miss White said, 'OK, class. It's break time. I'll see you in twenty minutes.'

In Michael's head, Andrew tells him not to listen to the boys who say horrible things to him. Michael finds the lessons easy and knows all the answers, but doesn't say much so that the others won't notice him.

[1] **though** however
[2] **notice** see

Egghead

'WE WANT MORE MEN. WE WANT MORE MEN.'

At break time, the boys shouted this, walking around the playground. They walked together. Boys joined them as they marched¹ around. It was like a very long chain². When the chain was long enough they would play a game together. It was very exciting. I tried to join the chain.

'WE WANT MORE MEN. WE WANT MORE MEN.'

'Get out, Freeman. Eggheads can't play,' said one boy.

'Yeah. Leave the chain now. We don't want you to play with us, Egghead,' said another.

So I left the chain. I sat in the corner of the playground, watching the other boys and girls play. They were having so much fun. Why couldn't I join? Why do I belong when I walk up my hill, but not here at my school? What did I do wrong?

'Don't worry,' said Andrew. 'You're doing nothing wrong. I'll think of something.'

'Thank goodness³ for Andrew,' I thought. He was always there for me. He's so important and he really wants me to be happy.

> The other boys don't let Michael play with them and he's very sad. He thinks he's done something wrong. Then in his head, Andrew tells him not to worry. Andrew always helps him in difficult moments like this one.

---

¹ **march** walk together in the same way
² **chain** look at the picture on page 25. The other boys are holding each other. This is a chain
³ **Thank goodness** Thank God

Michael Lacey Freeman

Michael is happy when school finishes so he can go home and read without being called horrible names. On the way home, he sees the other boys bullying David. They always call David 'Bacon' because he has a red face.

At lunchtime in the school dining hall, Andrew was still there, helping me. *'Be careful,'* he said. I was at the table, having my school dinner. *'That potato is hot.'*

'Thanks Andrew,' I said. Everybody tried to finish their potato very quickly. When it was cold it was impossible to eat. It tasted horrible and you have to finish all your dinner. You can only leave when you finish everything, so you have to eat the potato very quickly.

After lunch, we had a history lesson, then school finished at four o' clock. That was the best time of day for me. Finally, I could go home to my bedroom. I could read my books and nobody called me names. I was thinking about this when I heard some boys on the other side of the road. They were shouting something,

'Oink, Oink! It's Bacon[1],' said one voice.

'Bacon, piggy, piggy, piggy,' said another.

They were some boys from my class. They were shouting at David, a boy from another class. The boys in my class called him, 'Bacon.' David was just in front of me. He was bullied a lot, just like me, because he had a very red face, and he lived on a farm. People are bullied for the most stupid things. But at that moment I had a stupid idea. *'If I fight[2] David, the others will like me,'* I thought.

Michael is sad because he'd like to play with the other boys but they won't let him join them.

---

[1] **bacon**
[2] **fight** look at the picture of Michael and David on page 27. They're fighting

Michael Lacey Freeman

Michael fights with David because he wants the others to like him. Then he sees David's face and he understands that he's sad and afraid like him. Michael says he's sorry and the two become friends.

And so I ran up to David, and jumped on him. Then I held him down. This was my chance[1].

'Look,' said one of the boys on the other side of the road. 'Egghead has got him. Well done, Egghead!'

At first I was very happy. 'Maybe now they'll like me,' I thought. 'Maybe now, I'll belong.'

But then I turned and looked at David's face. It was the face of somebody who was always afraid. The face of somebody who was hated for no reason. It was a face like my face. 'Why am I doing this?' I thought. 'This is wrong.'

'I'm sorry, so sorry David. I don't know why I did that. Please forgive[2] me.'

Then David and I heard another boy from the other side of the road. 'Ha Ha Ha! Look at them. It's Egg and Bacon.' Egg and bacon looked at each other and at that moment we understood each other. At that moment we became friends.

> **Michael starts to fight with David, then he sees how afraid David is and he says he's sorry.**

Think
Have you ever done anything stupid and then felt sorry about it?

[1] **chance** a good moment to do something
[2] **forgive** you normally do this when someone says they're sorry

After-reading Activities • Chapter 1

Reading Comprehension

❶ Read these sentences and decide who's speaking.

> Andrew   A group of boys   Clive   Michael
> Mrs Jarvis   Miss White   ~~The Old Man~~

'Hello, Cherub.' ___The Old Man___

1 'Put your hat and scarf on. It's very cold out there.'
___

2 'Where were you? At the zoo?'
___

3 'OK, class. It's break time.'
___

4 'We want more men!'
___

5 'Be careful, that potato is hot.'
___

6 'I'm so sorry, David. I don't know why I did that.'
___

Grammar

❷ Look at the sentences and circle the correct word(s).

I hate (going) / *to go* to school.
1 There's an old man who always *sitting / sits* on the same bench.
2 'I have to *being / be* very careful. That's why I've got this walking stick.'
3 When I'm older I want *having / to have* a walking stick.
4 When I got to the top of the hill I stopped *feeling / to feel* happy.
5 'Don't listen to Kevin and Clive. They don't know what they're *talking / they talk* about.
4 How I'd like *to being / to be* in the woods now.

Reading A2 Key

3 **Complete this part of the story about Michael meeting David with one word in each space.**

Then I turned _and_ looked (**1**) ____ David's face. It (**2**) ____ the face of somebody (**3**) ____ was always afraid. The face of somebody who was hated for (**4**) ____ reason. It was a face (**5**) ____ my face. (**6**) '____ am I doing this?' I thought. 'This is wrong.'

Writing

21st Century Skills

4 **In Chapter 2, Michael talks about a day at school. Now answer these questions about your school day.**

1. Michael walks to school. How do you get to school?
2. Michael hates going to school because they bully him. Do you like school, or not?
3. Michael finds the lessons easy. What's your best subject? Why?
4. At break time, the boys and girls play in the playground. What do you do at break time?
5. Michael has lunch at school. Where do you have lunch?
6. Michael's lessons finish at 4 o'clock. When do your lessons finish?
7. Michael and David become friends. Who's your best friend?

Before-reading Activity

Prediction

5A **Now Michael has a friend. Do you think things will get better at school for Michael?**

1. ☐ Yes   2. ☐ No   3. ☐ Maybe

▶ 7 **5B** **Listen to track 7. Do you want to change your answer to exercise 5A? Explain why.**

Chapter 3

Egg and Bacon and the Invisible[1] Ball

▶ 6 *March 1973*

Finally, I've got a friend. A real friend. His name's David. Every day we play together at break time. The other children call us Egg & Bacon. But we pretend they're not there. The other day we made a promise[2].

'David, let's play together all the time. I'll never call you Bacon. Will you promise that you'll never call me Egghead?'

'I promise,' said David.

'What shall we do then?' I asked.

'Let's run,' said David.

David likes running, so at every break time we run round the playground. The playground is very big, but sometimes we even run round it ten times before we have to go back to the classroom. Ten times! Just imagine.

'We're going to run every day,' said David. One day, we'll run for our country. You'll see. We'll become famous, and then nobody will bully us anymore.'

That seemed like a very good idea, and so we ran. Every day we ran. When we ran we felt free. When I ran I forgot school. I forgot about all of my problems.

Michael and David become best friends and play together every day at school. They run round the playground lots of times because David says one day they can run for their country and become famous and then nobody will bully them anymore.

---

[1] **invisible** something that nobody can see
[2] **promise** say you're going to do something

Egghead

But things can change very quickly at school. One day, after running with David, I went back into the classroom. We were going to do geography.

'Graham, what's the capital of Sweden?' asked the teacher.

This was so easy, but not for Graham.

'Er, Copenhagen, no, Oslo, no, ... wait a minute ... Sweden! No! er... What was the question again, Miss?'

While Graham was changing the map of the world, Kevin said something in my ear.

'Poo, Egghead. All that running you do,' he said. 'Why do I have to sit next to you? Anyway, I read in the newspaper that it's bad for you to run too much. Your legs can break.'

It was always the same. Whatever[1] I did, someone had something bad to say about it. Could my legs really break? Probably not, but this was something I had to speak to David about.

'Really?' said David when I saw him. 'Our legs can break! Well, we have to stop then. We're running too much. And if it's dangerous...'

'What are we going to do now then?' I asked.

David didn't know about Andrew. Maybe he had a secret friend as well, but I didn't know for sure. At that moment, Andrew had an idea. David couldn't hear

Michael and David love running, but then they stop because another boy says that they can break their legs if they run too much.

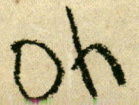

[1] **whatever** anything

Michael Lacey Freeman

it, but I could. Andrew said to me. *'Bring a ball to school. You can play football.'* What a brilliant idea! I didn't tell David about it. I wanted it to be a surprise.

The next day I brought a football to school. It was a beautiful ball. My Uncle Terry gave it to me for Christmas. It was red and white, like the colours of Arsenal, my favourite team.

▶ 7 David and I started to kick the ball around. I pretended to be an Arsenal player, Charlie George. He scores lots of goals for Arsenal, and David pretended to be Pat Jennings. He's a brilliant goalkeeper[1].

But soon, something incredible[2] happened. 'C'mon Egghead, pass the ball to me,' said a voice. It was Kevin. He started to play with us and then Clive came, and then some other boys. Soon there were about 20 children playing football with us, Egg and Bacon. I couldn't believe it. It was brilliant.

▶ 8 When lessons started again, Kevin said to me. 'Bring the ball tomorrow, Egghead. We'll play again.' So that's what I did. Soon we were playing football with the other boys every day.

But then one day, the fun stopped. We had to stop playing. It was all because of Mr Williams. He was the

Andrew gives Michael the idea of bringing a ball to school so he and David can play football. Then all the other boys want to play with them too. Michael is really happy about this.

The P. E. teacher says they can't play football in the playground.

[1] **goalkeeper** the person in a football team who can stop goals using their hands
[2] **incredible** a great surprise

Michael Lacey Freeman

The P.E. teacher stops their fun because he says it's too dangerous to play football at school, even when Michael brings a smaller, softer ball.

P.E. teacher[1]. One day, we started to play, but then he blew his whistle[2]. 'Stop boys!' he shouted. 'This is too dangerous. The ball is too hard. Play football in the park, but not at school.'

The other boys went away. I picked up the ball and put it in my bag. 'Oh well, that's another idea gone wrong,' I thought.

'Bring a smaller ball,' whispered[3] Andrew. I heard Andrew and smiled to myself.

The next day we were playing football again. This time with a much smaller ball. It was soft and difficult to see. But it was better than nothing. For three days we played with the small ball. At first, Mr Williams didn't say anything, but then he blew his whistle again.

'Stop boys. No balls in the playground. Put it away, Freeman.'

So that was that. 'Oh well,' I thought. 'At least you tried, Andrew. That's the end of football for us.' But Andrew had one more idea.

'Play with an invisible ball,' he said.

The boys were just about to go away, when I said 'Stop!' They all looked at me.

'What is it, Egghead?' asked Kevin.

'I've got a ball here, look. It's so small that even Mr

---

[1] **P.E. teacher** this teacher teaches sport. P.E. = physical education
[2] **blow a whistle** when you make a noise with this
[3] **whisper** speak quietly to someone so that the others can't hear you

Egghead

Williams can't see it.' I started to kick the invisible ball up and down.

'I knew it,' said Kevin. 'Egghead is crazy. What's he doing?'

Then I kicked the invisible ball to David, David kicked it to Clive, Clive kicked it to Kevin, and then something incredible happened. We were all playing invisible football, with an invisible ball.

It wasn't as good as a real ball. But it was still great fun.

Now when the boys shout 'We want more men,' they let us join the group. Now we're a part of something.

At the weekends I often go to David's house. His house isn't like mine. He lives on a farm. It's very exciting, and there are a lot of things to do.

We catch insects, and help David's dad to collect the eggs from the chickens. I'm glad Kevin and Clive aren't here when I do this. I also help to give the pig his food. His name's Hector. Sometimes David and I have tomato battles.

A tomato battle is really quite simple. David's mum and dad grow a lot of vegetables and they can't eat or sell them all. Some of them go bad. We use the bad tomatoes for our tomato battle. We both find a good

---

Andrew tells Michael to play with an invisible ball. At first the others think he's crazy, then they all start playing again. Now Michael and David are part of the group and they're happy. Michael also visits David on his farm at weekends.

Michael Lacey Freeman

Michael loves being on the farm with David. They have tomato battles too. His mum doesn't even get angry with him when she sees him all dirty after the tomato fight. She's happy he's had a good time.

hiding place and then we throw them at each other. One point for every time we hit each other. It's great fun.

When I came home after my first tomato fight I was worried. 'Now Mum will be really angry,' I thought. 'My clothes are so dirty, and they smell bad.' Mum was surprised when she saw me walk through the door. But she wasn't angry at all.

'Did you have a good time?' she asked.

'Yes thanks, Mum. It was great!' I replied[1].

She smiled. ■

> **Michael and David have great fun on the farm throwing bad tomatoes at each other.**

Think
When do your parents get angry with you?

[1] **reply** answer

After-reading Activities • Chapter 3

Reading and Writing

1 Complete the sentences with the correct names.

> Andrew ~~David~~ Kevin Miss White
> Mr Williams mum Uncle Terry

_____David_____ and Michael ran every day during break time.
1 _____ asked Graham a question.
2 _____ told Michael to bring a ball to school.
3 _____ gave Michael a ball for Christmas.
4 _____ and Clive played football with Michael and David.
5 _____ stopped them from playing football.
6 Michael's _____ smiled when she saw his dirty clothes.

Writing

2 Can you remember what Andrew says to Michael in this chapter? Complete the sentences.

1 Bring a ball _____ .
2 You can _____ .
3 Play with _____ .

Reading A2 Key

3 Complete the summary of Chapter 3 with one word in each space.

Michael and David soon _became_ friends. At first, (1) _____ ran together during break time. But after Kevin told Michael that running wasn't good for (2) _____, they stopped. After that, Michael and David (3) _____ know what to do. But Andrew had (4) _____ idea. He told Michael to bring a ball with (5) _____ to school. They played football, and soon the (6) _____ children wanted to play too.

Writing

4 **Do you think you know Michael well? Write some sentences about him.**

21st Century Skills

He reads books. He has...

Before-reading Activity

Listening

▶ 10 **5 A Listen to track 10 and answer the question.**

Why's Michael excited? What's he going to do at the weekend?

1. ☐ He's going out with his mother.
2. ☐ He's going on holiday.
3. ☐ He's going somewhere special.

5 B Listen again. Which places does Michael want to visit at the weekend? Tick (✓) the correct answers.

☐ an art gallery ☐ a park
☐ a fun fair ☐ a theatre
☐ a museum ☐ a zoo

Chapter 4

The Old Man

▶9 April 1973

'Are you ready to play invisible football?' I said one day to the other boys.

'No,' said Kevin. 'I'm tired of playing that game.'

'So am I,' said Clive, who always agreed with everything that Kevin said.

So that was the end of invisible football. They were bored with it and they were bored with me and David as well. There was nothing we could do.

'I was tired of playing with them anyway,' said David. But I didn't believe him. We were happy playing with the other boys. We felt like we belonged to the group. We felt important. But now we were just 'Egg and Bacon' again. We were alone.

'Well, if nobody wants to play with us anymore, we'll do something else,' I said.

'What?' asked David.

'I don't know.' Andrew didn't know either. But then I had an idea. 'Let's read some of our books. There are a lot of adventures in those stories. Maybe they'll give us some ideas.'

Michael and David are alone again because the other boys are bored playing with them. They don't know what to do. Then Michael has the idea of reading some of their books.

Egghead

So we read. We read during break time. We read at home. We took as many books as we could home with us from the school library, then we talked about what we read.

It was good to live inside those stories, and then to share them with David. We often sat on the grass at his farm and talked about the stories, while eating banana sandwiches.

'Hey, you know what?' I said one day.

'What?' asked David.

▶ 10 'It's my birthday next weekend. My dad asked me what I want for my birthday, and I said I wanted to go to London. Dad said I can bring a friend. Do you want to come with me?'

'Yessssss!' he shouted happily. 'Let's go to London. We can go to the zoo, and to the Natural History Museum. I'd really like to go there.'

'Me too,' I said. 'Let's do it.'

▶ 11 The next day was Monday. I didn't even care when the other children called me Egghead. All I could think about was London. What an adventure!

The week passed slowly, then Saturday arrived. The big day. Mum made me some sandwiches, and I put them in my bag.

Michael and David read a lot of books and talk about the stories. Then Michael invites David to go to London with him for his birthday. David is really happy about the idea.

Michael Lacey Freeman

'Have a great time,' said Mum. 'And put your coat on if it rains. I don't want you to get wet.'

'OK, Mum,' I said. And then I ran out of the door and Dad and I drove to David's house.

It was a wonderful day. David bought me a present. A plane. You had to make it yourself. The picture of it on the box looked really good. We visited the zoo first. I liked the monkeys best, but the tigers and lions were also really interesting. Then we went to Hyde Park. 'Let's go on a boat,' I said.

'Good idea,' said David.

We both tried to move the boat to the other side of the lake, but we weren't very good. We just went round and round in a circle. We weren't going anywhere. David and I started laughing, and soon we were very wet. I was happy that Mum couldn't see us. After half an hour a man started shouting at us. 'That's 30 minutes. Now you have to come back.' But it took a long time to get back to where the man was waiting. We weren't very good on the water, but it was fun.

After that we went to the National History Museum. It was a very old museum. The zoo was full of living animals, but this was full of dead things. There were lots of dinosaurs and all kinds of insects. It was very

Michael and David have great fun in London. They go to the zoo, then go on a boat in Hyde Park. They're not very good at moving the boat and they laugh a lot.

Michael and David are laughing a lot in the boat on the lake because they're going round in circles all the time.

Michael Lacey Freeman

interesting. The best bit was when we saw a little piece of the moon.

'Just imagine,' I said. 'This rock was on the moon. I'd like to go there one day.'

'Well, maybe for your next birthday,' said David smiling.

We got back from London quite late, but Mum was waiting for me at the door.

'Did you enjoy yourselves?' asked Mum

'Oh yes, Mum. We went to the zoo, then to Hyde Park, and then to the Natural History Museum. Oh, Mum. It was the best day ever.'

Mum seemed pleased. She smiled to herself. It was nice to see her so happy.

Soon it was Monday morning again. As usual, I walked up the hill. After such an exciting weekend it was difficult to think of school.

On my way up the hill I saw the old man, sitting in his usual place.

'Hello, Cherub,' he said, as he always did.

'Hello. You're always so nice to me,' I said. 'What's your name?'

'My name's Colin, but everybody calls me Tom.'

Michael's mum is happy when she sees that Michael enjoyed his day. Michael walks to school as usual on Monday morning and sees the old man again.

Egghead

'Pleased to meet you, Tom,' I said smiling. 'Why do you always sit here?'

'Well, it stops me feeling lonely, you know. Sitting here gives me a chance to meet people. People like you. I've always lived here on this street, you know. I've seen a lot of things in my time on this street.'

When I think about it, we meet different people every day. But we don't really know them. We never have the whole story. When we meet people it's like looking at a photograph. We only see them in that moment. We don't have a full picture of their lives. I just saw Tom as an old man. For me he was always an old man. But once he was young like me.

'Will you be here tomorrow?' I asked.

'Yes, of course,' said Tom.

'If I leave for school a little earlier, we could have a chat, if you like.'

'Well, bless your heart[1],' said Tom. 'Not many children are like you. You're special. Of course I'll be here. I'd like to know something about you too. I'll see you tomorrow then.'

'Ok, Tom,' I said. 'See you tomorrow. 'What a nice man,' I thought. 'And he called me special. Nobody has

Michael stops to talk to the old man everyone calls Tom. Michael decides he wants to learn more about him, and Tom is really happy that he'll have someone to talk to.

---

[1] **bless your heart** you say this to someone when they're kind

Michael Lacey Freeman

Tom says Michael isn't like other children - he's special. Michael is really happy about this and smiles even though he has to go to school.

ever called me special before, except Mum and Dad, but mums and dads always say things like that, even if it's not true. Well ... maybe I am special.' With that thought, and a smile on my face I went up the hill to begin another week of school.

Think
What can you learn by talking to your grandparents or other old people?

Michael stops to speak to Tom on his way to school and they decide to have a longer chat the next day.

After-reading Activities • Chapter 4

Reading Comprehension

1 Choose the correct answer - A or B.

Michael and David stopped playing football because
- **A** ☑ the other boys didn't want to play anymore.
- **B** ☐ they wanted to play basketball.

1 Michael and David read stories
- **A** ☐ because they wanted to do well at school.
- **B** ☐ to get ideas about what to do.

2 Michael and David went to London
- **A** ☐ with Michael's dad.
- **B** ☐ with David's dad.

3 What did Michael especially like about the Natural History Museum?
- **A** ☐ The insects
- **B** ☐ A rock from the moon

4 When Michael got home his mum was
- **A** ☐ angry.
- **B** ☐ happy.

Pair Work

21st Century Skills

2A Where do Michael and David see these signs? Work with a partner and match the signs with the right place.

Places
1. ☐ The zoo
2. ☐ Hyde Park
3. ☐ The Natural History Museum

Signs
- **A** Do not touch
- **B** Monkey House
- **C** Don't play football on the grass
- **D** Don't give food to the animals
- **E** Boats £1 for the day

2B Now think of some more signs you see at school, in shops or on roads, and draw them with your partner.

Reading A2 Key

3 Complete this part from Chapter 4 with one word for each space.

'Are you ready ___to___ play invisible football?' I said **(1)** _____ the other boys. 'No', said Kevin. 'I'm tired **(2)** _____ playing this game. '**(3)** _____ am I,' said Clive, **(4)** _____ always agreed **(5)** _____ everything that Kevin said. So that was the end **(6)** _____ invisible football.

Before-reading Activity
Listening

▶ 12 **4A** **Listen to track 12. Who's Michael speaking to?**

4B **Put the missing parts of the conversation in the right place. Then listen again to see if you're correct.**

> Well, what's wrong with that name?
> Egghead means something else   they always call me names
> Clever! Me! Clever?   It means clever, really clever
> ~~'It means little angel'~~

'Why do you call me Cherub?' I asked.
'It means little angel.'
'I'm no angel. The other children at school **(1)** _____ . But not nice names like that.'
'What do they call you then,' asked Tom.
'Egghead mostly.'
'Egghead. I see. **(2)** _____ '
I started to explain, but he soon stopped me. 'I've never noticed that. That's not important. But **(3)** _____ .'
'What does it mean?' I asked.
'**(4)** _____ . It's a good word for you. You seem like a very clever boy to me.'
I didn't know that Egghead had two meanings. **(5)** _____ .

Chapter 5

Tom's Story

▶ 12   The next morning I got up early to speak to Tom. I had a lot of questions.

'Why do you call me Cherub?' I asked.

'It means little angel.'

'I'm no angel. The other children at school always call me names. But not nice names like that.'

'What do they call you then?' asked Tom.

'Egghead mostly.'

'Egghead. I see. Well, what's wrong with that name?'

I started to explain, but he soon stopped me. 'I've never noticed that. That's not important. But Egghead means something else.'

'What does it mean?' I asked.

'It means clever, really clever. It's a good word for you. You seem¹ like a very clever boy to me.'

I didn't know that Egghead had two meanings. Clever! Me! Clever? ■

▶ 13   'Of course you're clever,' said Andrew. 'You're good at your schoolwork. You always answer the teacher's questions. In fact, school work is quite easy for you.'

Tom tells Michael that 'Egghead' means clever. Michael is surprised. He doesn't think of himself as being clever.

¹ **seem** give the idea that

Egghead

'Thank you Andrew,' I said silently[1].

I said goodbye to Tom and promised to see him the next day. I went to school feeling much happier.

At school that day, there was a French test. All the children had to recite the verb, *to be*. I knew all the answers. '*Je suis, Tu es, Il est.*' I looked around the class. Kevin and Clive weren't doing very well. They started to move their mouth up and down but you could tell that they didn't really know the answers. Maybe Tom was right. I am quite clever.

Every morning I went to speak to Tom. And every morning we had a really nice chat. It made me feel much better about going to school.

One day Tom said to me, 'Michael, does it make you sad when the children call you names?'

'Yes, it does,' I answered. 'It hurts[2] me inside. It makes me feel alone. I've got a friend, David – he knows how I feel, he's my only real friend at school.'

'You know,' said Tom. 'These children who call you names don't really know you. You shouldn't worry about what they say.'

'But it's difficult not to worry, and feel sad' I said.

'Just remember, they don't know you,' said Tom. 'So, if they don't know you, what they say isn't important. Don't

> Tom's words help Michael to feel better about school and he starts to think that maybe he is clever. Tom tells him not to worry about what the other children say, but Michael says it's hard not to feel sad.

---

[1] **silently** (here) inside his head, without actually saying the words
[2] **hurt** when something makes you feel bad

Michael Lacey Freeman

Tom says it isn't important what the children call Michael because they don't really know him.

let it hurt you inside. Remember, everybody who cares about you, and knows you, your mum and dad, David, and me, don't call you names. The others aren't important.'

'But they're so horrible to me.'

'Well, just try and remember what I said, then you'll feel better. You'll see. I know it's difficult to understand, but let me tell you a story. See that house there?'

'Which one? That one?' I asked, pointing to the house across the street.

Tom tells Michael that during the war he saved three children after their house was bombed. Nobody remembers now and Tom doesn't know many people anymore, so he likes talking to Michael. Michael is really surprised by Tom's story.

'Yes, that one. Well, during the war, a bomb[1] fell on that house and I went in. It was on fire. People were frightened. There were three children. I got them out. They were alive[2]. They're older now. They've moved on, to a different place. All the people I knew have all gone. Moved away to new lives. Nobody remembers me. I don't know most of the people who live here now. It's nice to see a friendly face like yours.' 'Wow!' I said. That's all I could say. It was incredible. I didn't know anything about this. 'People should know about things like this,' I said. 'Why don't they know? You're a hero[3].'

'People don't want to know about the past,' said

---

[1] **bomb**
[2] **alive** not dead
[3] **hero** heroes do something for other people without worrying about themselves

Egghead

Tom. 'They're too busy with their lives to worry about me. They just think I'm a useless[1] old man. But I don't get angry about it. The people who live here now don't know me. So, how can I be angry with them?'

'Well,' I thought, 'if Tom can do that why can't I? At least I can try.'

That day at school, I had a swimming lesson. I like swimming. The other kids bullied me, as always, 'Eggheads can't swim, their heads are too big,' was what they said. But when I'm swimming I can put my head under the water. It's so quiet there. I can see all the arms and legs of the other boys, but I can't hear them. Under the water I thought of what Tom said to me. 'They don't know me.'

When the lesson finished, I went into the changing room. The next class was getting ready to swim. When they saw me come in they started to sing,

'THEY CALL HIM EGGHEAD, HE HAS THE BIGGEST HEAD YOU'VE EVER SEEN.'

I looked at them, and again I remembered what Tom said. I had my mum and my dad, Andrew, David and now Tom. They loved me.

Michael thinks that if Tom doesn't get angry or sad because people don't really know him, he can do the same. While he's swimming he forgets about the others, but when he comes out, the others sing a horrible song about him having a big head.

---

[1] **useless** of no use for anything

Michael Lacey Freeman

For the first time I thought, 'I don't need them. They can say what they want. I forgive them because they only have a photograph of me. They don't really know me, just like I didn't know Tom at first. They don't know the whole story.'

I smiled to myself. Then a strange thing happened.

The singing stopped.

I got dressed quickly. It was break time and I wanted to tell David what happened.

'They stopped singing, you say?' said David.

'Yes. I know they won't stop forever,' I said. 'They never stop. But the important thing is, I don't care anymore. Try and do the same thing. That's all I'm saying.'

'OK,' said David. 'I'll try. But it's not going to be easy.'

After break time we had an English lesson. But we had quite a surprise. There was a new teacher. Her name was Mrs Hewitt. She had curly brown hair and a kind face. I knew I was going to like her a lot.

'OK, class,' said Mrs Hewitt. 'I don't know you, and I want to learn something about you. That's why I want you to do some writing for me.'

Michael remembers Tom's words and he doesn't care anymore if the other children are horrible to him. They don't really know him. He smiles and they stop singing. He tells David to try and not care, like him.

Michael is in the swimming pool. He loves swimming because under the water it's quiet and he can't hear the horrible things that the others say about him.

Michael Lacey Freeman

The new English teacher, Mrs Hewitt, tells them to write about an important person in their life. The person who writes the best story will read it in front of the school the following week. Michael is excited about this idea.

'Oh No!' said the class.

'Oh yes,' said Mrs Hewitt. It's a good way to get to know you better. So I want you to write about an important person in your life. The best essay[1] will get a prize[2].

'What's the prize, Miss?' asked Sally.

'He or she will read their essay in front of the school next week.'

I was very excited. This was the best prize ever. When school finished I wanted to speak to Andrew about it. 'Just think, Andrew, to read my essay in front of the school. I'd really like that. If I win, I can tell everybody about a person who's important to me. Writing about somebody is like telling a story, don't you think? A story of their life. We all have a story, you know. It's just that often people don't want to hear it. But when they do, they realise[3] how interesting it's.'

'Yes, you're right Michael. We all have a story. Well, whose story do you want to tell?' asked Andrew.

'I'm not sure.' I said. 'I have to think for a moment.'

---

[1] **essay** a piece of writing on a particular subject
[2] **prize** something special that you win in a competition
[3] **realise** understand

Egghead

'*Let's think together then,*' said Andrew.

I sat on my bed with Andrew, and I thought about all the people I know. After two or three minutes, I had an idea. '*I know who I can write about,*' I said.

'*So do I,*' said Andrew. Andrew and I thought of the same thing. We both thought of the same person. '*I know Andrew,*' I said. '*I was thinking of him as well.*' '*Let's write about him. I'll help you if you want,*' said Andrew. Who was this person? I think you know. ⏹

Michael talks to Andrew and they both decide on the same person to write about.

Think
Do you like writing stories? Why / Why not?

After-reading Activities • Chapter 5

Reading Comprehension

1 Tick (✓) the things that Michael learns about the old man in this chapter.

- [✓] His real name
- 1 [ ] His age
- 2 [ ] Where he lives
- 3 [ ] His job
- 4 [ ] His friends
- 5 [ ] What he thinks of Michael
- 6 [ ] His hobbies

Reading A2 Key

2 Complete what Tom says to Michael with one word in each space.

These children who call _you_ names (**1**) _____ really know you. You shouldn't worry (**2**) _____ what they say. (**3**) _____ they don't know you, what they say (**4**) _____ important. Remember, everybody (**5**) _____ cares about you, and knows you, your mum and dad, David and (**6**) _____, don't call you names. The others aren't important.

Writing

21st Century Skills

3 In Chapter 5, the teacher tells each member of the class to write about somebody important in their life. Write about somebody important in your life. Answer the questions to help you.

1. Who is the person?
2. How long have you known this person?
3. Why have you chosen to write about them?
4. What have you learnt from this person?
5. How often do you see this person?
6. What do you do together?

Pair Work

4 **Work with a partner. Ask him / her the following questions, then match the answers to the questions to see if you were right.**

Questions
1. [c] What's different about the English lesson?
2. [ ] What does Michael think of Mrs Hewitt?
3. [ ] What exercise did Mrs Hewitt ask the class to do?
4. [ ] What did the class have to write about?
5. [ ] What's special about this exercise?

Answers
a They had to write an essay.
b The best essay will get a prize.
c There's a new teacher.
d An important person in their life.
e He thinks she's very kind.

Before-reading Activity

Prediction

5 **Try to guess what's going to happen.**

1. Why does Michael want to win the prize?
    a [ ] So that everybody will know that Tom is a hero.
    b [ ] So that the other children won't bully him anymore.
2. Who do you think will help a little bit Michael with the essay?
    a [ ] Mrs Hevitt
    b [ ] Andrew
3. Do you think he'll win the prize?
    a [ ] Yes
    b [ ] No

Chapter 6

The Prize

▶ 14 The next day, Mrs Hewitt gave us one hour to write. Andrew helped me with some words, but I did most of it by myself. I wrote so much and the hour passed very quickly.

'OK, class. Put your pens down. I'll have a look at your work during the weekend.'

It was the weekend. My favourite time of the week. 'I'll probably go and see David at the farm,' I thought. 'I've got lots of books to read.' But the first thing I wanted to do on Saturday morning was to see Tom.

On Saturday morning I got up early and went up the hill.

'Where are you going?' asked Mum.

'Erm... I'm going to see a friend,' I said.

'Who? David?' asked Mum.

'No, somebody else.'

Mum smiled to herself as I ran out of the door.

'Tom, there you are,' I said.

'Good morning, Cherub. What are you doing here? There's no school today.'

'I know, but I wanted to speak to you. I had to

Michael writes a lot in the hour and then it's the weekend and he goes and sees Tom early even if it's Saturday. Tom is surprised to see him.

Egghead

write something at school yesterday. It was an essay, and I wrote about you.'

'About me. Why?'

'Because I had to write about somebody who's important to me.'

'Well, bless your heart, Michael. That's very nice of you. I'd like to read it.'

'You will one day, and maybe lots of other people will hear your story, too.'

I wanted to win this prize so badly. For the first time I wanted the weekend to end quickly. I wanted to go back to school to see if Mrs Hewitt liked my essay.

On Monday morning, I ran up the hill. I stopped to say hello to Tom, and then I went to school.

The first lesson was art. I drew the road, and the hill that I walked up every day. My picture had a lot of trees and beautiful flowers in it. The sky was blue, and in the distance[1], you could see the bench where Tom sat.

The next lesson was science. I tried to listen to the lesson, but I couldn't stop thinking about the essay. I looked out of the window. The school flag[2] was moving around in the wind. I like the wind. It comes from nowhere. You can't see it, but it's so strong. In a way,

Tom is happy to hear that Michael has written about him. Michael really wants to win the prize so that everyone can hear the story about Tom.

---

[1] **in the distance** far away
[2] **flag**

Michael Lacey Freeman

looking at the flag moving helped me to see the wind. I felt a little bit like the flag. Things happen to me, and I have no control¹. Just like the flag. 'Who knows,' I thought, 'where the wind will take me?'

At break time, I talked to David. '"We've got English next. I hope I win, David. I really want to win.'

'Well, don't be too sad if you don't win. You told me about that poem, 'The Monster Horse.' Maybe they won't let you read it.'

'Mrs Hewitt is different. I know she'll like what I wrote. I know,' I said.

Finally it was time for English. It was the last lesson of the day. I waited for Mrs Hewitt to begin.

'Class, I read your work, and corrected it.' She looked around the classroom, and then she began giving the work back. She said something to everyone. 'Not bad,' she said to Sally. 'Could do better,' she said to Graham. 'This isn't good enough, you didn't even try,'

Michael feels a bit like the flag moving in the wind because he feels he has no control over what happens to him.

Michael tells David that Mrs Hewitt is different from the last teacher and that she'll like what he wrote. Michael waits while the teacher gives everyone back their essays.

¹ **control** when you can decide what to do

Egghead

she said to Clive. 'I can't even read your writing,' she said to Kevin. Then she arrived in front of me. I didn't want to look at her. I kept my head down. But Mrs Hewitt waited until I looked up. She looked at me and smiled. 'Yours is the best,' she said. 'Keep it that way.'

'So, class, Michael will read his essay at the school assembly next week,' said Mrs Hewitt.

Everybody looked at me. I waited for somebody to say something bad, but nobody did. At the end of the class, I ran all the way home. I couldn't wait to get home to tell Mum.

'Mum! Mum! First prize – the essay – the old man, I mean Tom – I have to tell him – I'm going to read it to everyone.'

'Slow down,' said Mum. 'Now, tell me. What are you talking about?'

I told Mum everything, about Tom, and the essay,

Mrs Hewitt says Michael's essay was the best so he'll read it to everyone at the school assembly. Nobody in the class says anything bad to him.

When Michael gets home, he tells his mum everything about Tom and the essay, about Andrew and how the other children at school bully him. He feels great after telling her everything and he can't wait to tell Tom that his story was the best.

Michael Lacey Freeman

In his room, Michael wants to tell Andrew all about the assembly that morning. Andrew hasn't spoken to him all day. His mum, Tom and a man taking photographs were also at the assembly.

and what Mrs Hewitt said. I also told her about Andrew. I even told her about how the other children bullied me. It felt so good to be able to tell my mum everything.

Mum smiled. 'Oh Michael. Your father and I love you so much. We always have and we always will.' Then she took me in her arms and gave me the biggest kiss ever.

It's the evening after the school assembly. I'm writing this in my bedroom. I read my essay to the school this morning, and I really want to speak to Andrew about it.

'Andrew, I read the essay this morning. You haven't spoken to me today. Why's that? Were you at school today? Did you hear me read the essay?'

'I went to the front of the hall with my essay. I was ready to tell everybody about Tom. I looked out at the people in front of me. There was my class, and boys and girls from other classes. Then I saw David. He smiled at me, and gave me a big Thumbs Up sign[1]. But you won't believe who I saw next. It was my mum – she was there! "What's she doing here?" I thought. Then I was even more surprised. I saw that Tom was standing next to her and there was a man taking photographs. It was all very strange.'

'I read the essay very well. We wrote it together,

---

[1] **thumbs up sign**

Egghead

remember? Even if you weren't there to help me, I didn't make any mistakes. Mrs Hewitt told me not to speak too fast and to be very clear. So I tried to read it slowly and clearly. I told them all about Tom during the war, and what he did for those children. I told them that Tom was a hero, and that people shouldn't forget him.'

At the end, everybody clapped[1], and when I say everybody, I mean everybody – even Kevin and Clive. I couldn't believe it. I really couldn't.'

'But the best thing of all was that I could see Mum and Tom smiling at me. They were really happy.'

'You know what? Tom is going to be in the local newspaper. Mum phoned them to tell them about Tom, and they came to the school that day to speak to him. That's why the man was there – taking photographs. They're writing an article[2] about him. The title of the article is going to be, "Tom Matthews – Local Hero." There will be photos and the article will talk about Tom's life. Oh, Andrew, did you hear me speak? Why weren't you there? Why didn't you speak to me? Andrew, Andrew!

Andrew are you there?'

I don't know where Andrew is. Why isn't he speaking

> Michael tells Andrew that everybody loved the story about Tom and the newspaper is going to write an article about him. But Michael can't understand why Andrew wasn't there.

[1] **clap** people in a theatre do this with their hands at the end of a performance to show they enjoyed themselves.
[2] **article** a story in a newspaper

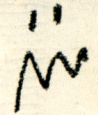# Michael Lacey Freeman

Michael can't hear Andrew in his head anymore. He doesn't need him like he did before, but he'll always remember how he helped him.

to me at the moment? Perhaps he thinks I don't need him anymore. Andrew has been so important to me, and I'll never forget him. But maybe he's right. I miss him, but I don't need him so much anymore. Maybe he's busy helping somebody else now.

Maybe he's helping you.

Think
Would you like a 'special friend' like Andrew? Why / Why not?

> In class, Mrs Hewitt gives everyone back their essays and says that Michael's is the best.

After-reading Activities • Chapter 6

Reading Comprehension

1 Put the events in the story in the right order.

a ☐ Michael tells his mum everything.
b ☐ Michael goes to the science lesson.
c ☐ 1 Michael does the essay.
d ☐ Michael goes to his English lesson.
e ☐ Michael tells Tom about his essay.
f ☐ Michael speaks to Andrew in his bedroom.
g ☐ Mrs Hewitt tells Michael that his essay is the best.

2 Connect the first part of a sentence in column A with the second part in column B.

Column A

1 ☐ At the weekend Michael wanted to see David but
2 ☐ Michael wrote the essay about Tom because
3 ☐ The first lesson on Monday morning was art and
4 ☐ Sometimes Michael felt like a flag because
5 ☐ Michael had to wait for the English lesson because
6 ☐ Mrs Hewitt said to the class, 'I have read your work and

Column B

a he wanted people to know that he was a hero.
b corrected it.'
c it was the last lesson of the day.
d he also wanted to speak to Tom.
e Michael drew a picture of his road.
f things happened to him and he had no control.

Reading and Writing

3 Decide who's speaking to Michael.

> Mum (x2)   Tom   David   Mrs Hewitt

Where are you going? _Mum_
1 What are you doing here? There's no school today. _____
2 Don't be too sad if you don't win. _____
3 Yours is the best. Keep it that way. _____
4 Slow down. Now tell me what you're talking about. _____

Reading A2 Key

4 Complete the first part of Michael's speech about Tom with one word in each space.

Good afternoon. Today, I'm going to (**1**) _____ you about a friend of (**2**) _____. I see him (**3**) _____ day when I walk to school. He always smiles (**4**) _____ me and is always friendly. He's quite old and a lot of people (**5**) _____ notice him. But this man is a hero. His name is Tom and (**6**) _____ is his story.

Writing and Reading

21st Century Skills

5A What do you think of the ending of the story? Write short answers to these questions.

1 ☐ The ending is happy because _____
2 ☐ The ending is sad because _____
3 ☐ Andrew isn't there anymore because _____

5B This is a true story, and it doesn't end here. Read pages 70-71 to find out more about Michael.

Focus on...

Michael Lacey Freeman

Hello. My name's Michael. Thank you for reading my story. It means a lot to me. I was that young boy in 1973 and that young boy is still with me. I still remember him.
Now, so many years later, I wanted to write a story about that part of my life. I wanted to share my story with you.

A Happy Ending

My life as Egghead made me stronger. It helped me to understand people and try to listen to their story. Inside all of us there's a very interesting story.
When I was called names at school I hated myself. I thought that nobody liked me. I felt alone. Do you sometimes have that feeling? Well, if you do, just remember Tom's words. 'They don't know you.' If you've read this story, and you're bullied at school, I want you to know something. There will be a happy ending to your story.
Thanks to my mum, David, Tom, Mrs Hewitt, and of course Andrew, I learnt to know and like myself. They taught me so many things. Thanks to them I became a better person. There's one more thing I'd like to say. If you bully someone stop for a moment and think. Every time you bully somebody it makes you smaller.
It doesn't give you anything. It takes something away.

A True Story

Egghead is a story, a true story, a story about my life. But of course, it's not the whole story. There were many more moments when I laughed, when I was happy, and there were also many moments when I cried. I learnt a lot from that experience: how to give, how to share, but most of all I learnt that inside all of us there's a story. When I meet someone new, I want to know the whole story, don't you?

Discussion

Read what Michael writes in the story again. Do you think he was right?

'I never tell Mum and Dad about school. I want to tell them, but I don't want them to know that all the other children call me Egghead. Then maybe they'll call me Egghead as well.'

Focus on...
Bullying

'People are bullied for the most stupid things.'

There's a bully at school. He hits me and kicks me, almost every day. I don't know why he does it. What have I done wrong?

The other children call me names. It hurts me inside. It makes me feel so alone. I just want to be like the other boys and girls in my class.

I know the other children say bad things about me. They talk about me when I'm not there. They laugh when I come into the classroom.
I don't know what they're laughing about. They won't tell me.

I don't use social media, or an email account. The other children put photos of me there, and write bad things. Why do they do this?
They don't know me. They don't know how much it hurts.

Here are some people who had a difficult time at school because of bullying.

Demi Lovato

Prince Harry

Christina Aguilera

Tom Cruise

Bill Clinton

Kate Winslet

Daniel Radcliffe

Lady Gaga

Justin Timberlake

Rihanna

Michael Phelps

Barack Obama

Robert Pattison

Taylor Swift

Steven Spielberg

Madonna

Focus on...

School in Britain

In 1973, there was no Internet or email. People had to communicate with each other in different ways. People had to write letters. When Michael was at school he had a penfriend from France. His name was Claude. A penfriend is a friend who lives in a another town or country. Read what Michael writes to Claude about his school. Think of the school in your country and answer the questions that Michael asks Claude. Some school rules haven't changed since 1973 as these messages show you.

> Dear Claude,
> I like school, but I don't like going to school. Does that seem strange?
> Well, I like the teachers, and I learn lots of interesting things. But the other children bully me. They call me names. I don't like that. Do you have bullies at your school?

> Dear Claude,
> At school we have to wear a uniform.
> We have to wear it every day. We can't wear what we like.
> My uniform is red.
> Do you have to wear a school uniform?

Dear Claude,
I go to school from Monday to Friday. The weekends are free. The school day is very long. It begins at nine in the morning and ends at four in the afternoon. But don't worry, we have breaks, and an hour for lunch. I'm happy that I don't have to go to school at the weekend. Do you have to go to school on Saturdays?

Dear Claude,
I have lunch in the school canteen. The food isn't very good, but I like it when they make apple pie. Where do you have lunch?

Dear Claude
There are lots of subjects at school: maths, history, science, English, art and French. French is very difficult - not for you, of course!
Do you study English at school?

Dear Claude,
My favourite teacher is Mrs Hewitt. She's very clever and kind. Do you have a favourite teacher?

Focus on...

London - Places

In the story, Michael went to London. He visited London Zoo, The Natural History Museum, and Hyde Park. All of these places have a story to tell of their own.

London Zoo was the world's first scientific zoo. It opened on 27th April, 1828. At the beginning, it was difficult to look after the animals. People didn't know much about how to care for animals at that time. It was also difficult to control the animals. Sometimes animals escaped into the park nearby. In the first, year the zoo had 627 animals and 112,000 visitors. The zoo grew over the years and now millions of people from all over the world visit visit it. There are 1.1 million visitors a year, and nearly 17,000 animals there.

The Natural History Museum

The museum opened in April 1881 because the government decided that they needed a new building for its growing natural history collection. The building is famous for its dinosaur collection. Lots of children go to see them. There are also lots of things that you can see that the famous scientist, Charles Darwin, collected. You can also see a piece of the moon, just like Michael did in the story. It was a present from the President of the U.S.A., Richard Nixon, in 1973.

Hyde Park

King Henry the Eighth bought the park in 1536, but he wanted to use it for himself. It was another King, Charles the First, who opened the park to the public in 1637.
In the 1730s, Queen Caroline made the lake where Michael and David go on a boat. The lake is called, 'The Serpentine.'
Now, the park is open from early in the morning until midnight. It's visited by millions of tourists and people from London. It's a great place to relax, and get away from the crowds.

1 What other places in London do you know? Match a word in column A with a word in column B

	Column A		Column B
1	☐ Buckingham	a	Ben
2	☐ Big	b	Eye
3	☐ Trafalgar	c	Square
4	☐ Covent	d	Garden
5	☐ London	e	Palace
6	☐ Piccadilly	f	Circus

2 Which three places would you most like to visit?

Test Yourself

Use the words below to complete the sentences. You don't need to use all of the words.

> Andrew   friend   friends   ~~The Railway Children~~
> hot chocolate   hot milk   Men   Bacon   English
> tomato   running   invisible   History   Mr Williams
> Miss White   David   Treasure Island   boat   train   poem
> sausage   potato   science   Park
> hero   diary   school   class   essay

Michael's favourite book was *The Railway Children*.
1 Michael drinks _____ on Sunday evenings.
2 Michael read the title of a _____ in front of the school assembly.
3 Complete the sentence, 'We Want More _____.
4 The other children called Michael, 'Egghead,' and David _____.
5 _____ stopped Michael and the other boys from playing football.
6 At the farm, Michael and David had _____ battles.
7 Michael went to the Natural _____ Museum for his birthday.
8 Michael and David went on a boat in Hyde _____.
9 Michael really liked his new _____ teacher, Mrs Hewitt.
10 Mrs Hewitt asked the class to write an _____.
11 Michael read it in front of the _____.
12 Michael told the school that Tom was a _____.
13 At the end of the story, Michael doesn't know where _____ is.

Syllabus

Topics
School
Family
Friendship
Emotions

Verbs
Present perfect simple, present simple, present continuous, past simple, past continuous, future with *going* to, *will* for future reference, promises and predicitons.
Can for ability and permission, *could* for past ability, requests and suggestions
First conditional
Must/have to for obligation, *should* for advice, shall (suggestions and offers)
Common phrasal verbs

Teen ELi Readers

Stage 1
Maureen Simpson, *In Search of a Missing Friend*
Charles Dickens, *Oliver Twist*
Geoffrey Chaucer, *The Canterbury Tales*
Janet Borsbey & Ruth Swan, *The Boat Race Mystery*
Lucy Maud Montgomery, *Anne of Green Gables*
Mark Twain, *A Connecticut Yankee in King Arthur's Court*
Mark Twain, *The Adventures of Huckleberry Finn*
Angela Tomkinson, *Great Friends!*
Edith Nesbit, *The Railway Children*
Eleanor H. Porter, *Pollyanna*
Anna Sewell, *Black Beauty*
Kenneth Grahame, *The Wind in the Willows*

Stage 2
Elizabeth Ferretti, *Dear Diary...*
Angela Tomkinson, *Loving London*
Mark Twain, *The Adventures of Tom Sawyer*
Mary Flagan, *The Egyptian Souvenir*
Maria Luisa Banfi, *A Faraway World*
Frances Hodgson Burnett, *The Secret Garden*
Robert Louis Stevenson, *Treasure Island*
Elizabeth Ferretti, *Adventure at Haydon Point*
William Shakespeare, *The Tempest*
Angela Tomkinson, *Enjoy New York*
Frances Hodgson Burnett, *Little Lord Fauntleroy*
Michael Lacey Freeman, *Egghead*
Michael Lacey Freeman, *Dot to Dot*
Silvana Sardi, *The Boy with the Red Balloon*
Silvana Sardi, *Scotland is Magic!*
Silvana Sardi, *Garpur: My Iceland*
Silvana Sardi, *Follow your Dreams*
Gabriele Rebagliati, *Naoko: My Japan*

Stage 3
Anna Claudia Ramos, *Expedition Brazil*
Charles Dickens, *David Copperfield*
Mary Flagan, *Val's Diary*
Maureen Simpson, *Destination Karminia*
Anonymous, *Robin Hood*
Jack London, *The Call of the Wild*
Louisa May Alcott, *Little Women*
Gordon Gamlin, *Allan: My Vancouver*